IT'S TIME TO LEARN ABOUT CLAMS

It's Time to Learn about Clams

Walter the Educator

Silent King Books
A WhichHead Entertainment Imprint

Copyright © 2025 by Walter the Educator

All rights reserved. No part of this book may be reproduced in any manner whatsoever without written per- mission except in the case of brief quotations embodied in critical articles and reviews.

First Printing, 2024

Disclaimer

This book is a literary work; the story is not about specific persons, locations, situations, and/or circumstances unless mentioned in a historical context. Any resemblance to real persons, locations, situations, and/or circumstances is coincidental. This book is for entertainment and informational purposes only. The author and publisher offer this information without warranties expressed or implied. No matter the grounds, neither the author nor the publisher will be accountable for any losses, injuries, or other damages caused by the reader's use of this book. The use of this book acknowledges an understanding and acceptance of this disclaimer.

It's Time to Learn about Clams is a collectible early learning book by Walter the Educator suitable for all ages belonging to Walter the Educator's Time to Eat Book Series. Collect more books at WaltertheEducator.com

USE THE EXTRA SPACE TO TAKE NOTES AND DOCUMENT YOUR MEMORIES

CLAMS

Down in the sea where the waters are blue,

It's Time to Learn about

Clams

A clever little clam had a home with a view.

He lived in the sand where it's cozy and tight,

Snuggled up safely both day and night.

His shell was as shiny as a pearl in the sun,

It opened and closed when it wanted some fun.

He had tiny eyes that could barely peep,

Watching the fish as they wiggled and leap.

He breathed in the water through tiny small gills,

Filtering food with very few spills.

He loved to stay hidden when sharks came to see,

Tucked in his shell as snug as can be.

When bubbles rose up in a beautiful dance,

The clam watched with joy from his watery stance.

Seaweed would sway and tickle his toes,

As jellyfish floated like soft, glowy bows.

It's Time to Learn about

Clams

His friends were the crabs with their clickety claws,

And the shy little fish with their silvery jaws.

He opened his shell to munch on some plankton,

The clam felt so happy and warm deep inside.

Sometimes a seahorse would come say hello,

Twisting and twirling, putting on a show.

The clam never hurried, he took life slow,

Happy and peaceful wherever he'd go.

His house was a treasure of shells and fine sand,

A sweet little kingdom so perfectly planned.

At night when the stars shimmered up in the sky,

He dreamed of the ocean and how he could fly.

He imagined his shell like a shiny balloon,

It's Time to Learn about

Clams

Sailing past dolphins and waving at the moon.

But clams are for digging and burrowing deep,

So he stayed in his bed and drifted to sleep.

With soft salty waves to sing him a song,

The clam closed his shell and snuggled along.

Dreaming of corals and rainbows of fish,

Happy and safe, as snug as you wish.

Down in the sea where the currents still hum,

It's Time to Learn about

Clams

Sleeps our dear clam till the morning will come.

ABOUT THE CREATOR

Walter the Educator is one of the pseudonyms for Walter Anderson. Formally educated in Chemistry, Business, and Education, he is an educator, an author, a diverse entrepreneur, and he is the son of a disabled war veteran. "Walter the Educator" shares his time between educating and creating. He holds interests and owns several creative projects that entertain, enlighten, enhance, and educate, hoping to inspire and motivate you. Follow, find new works, and stay up to date with Walter the Educator™

at WaltertheEducator.com

www.ingramcontent.com/pod-product-compliance
Lightning Source LLC
LaVergne TN
LVHW051920060526
838201LV00060B/4091